S0-DXK-459

1960s Racing Car

Viking Longship

freight Train

Spy Plane

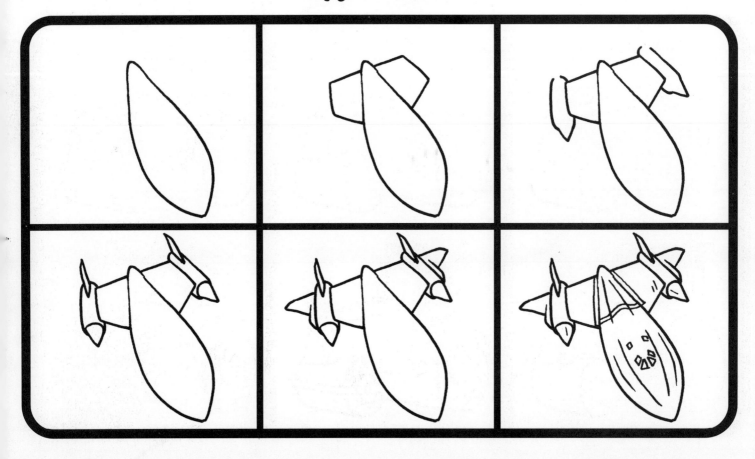

Formula 1 Racing Car

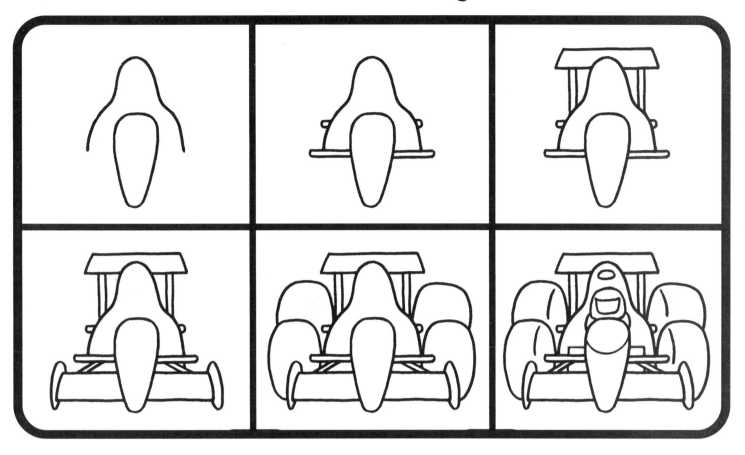

Road Roller

Cruise Ship

Chopper Bike

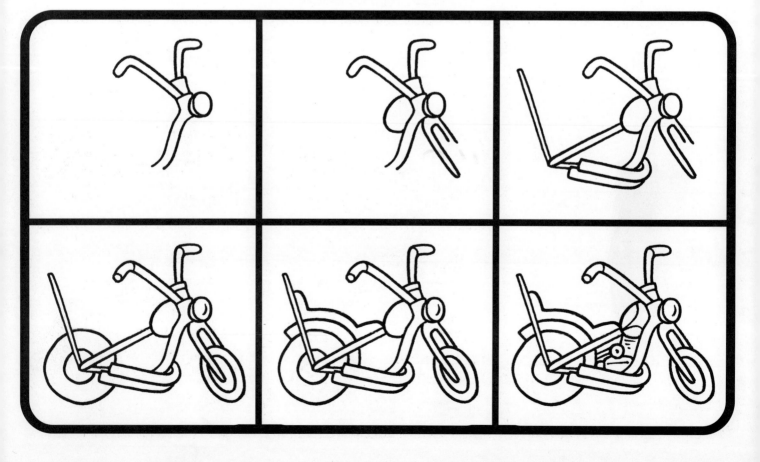

747 Jumbo Jet

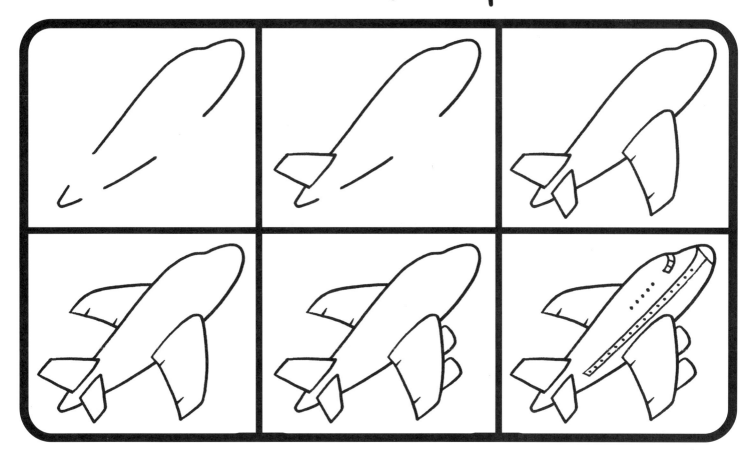

Custom Car

Mini

Digger

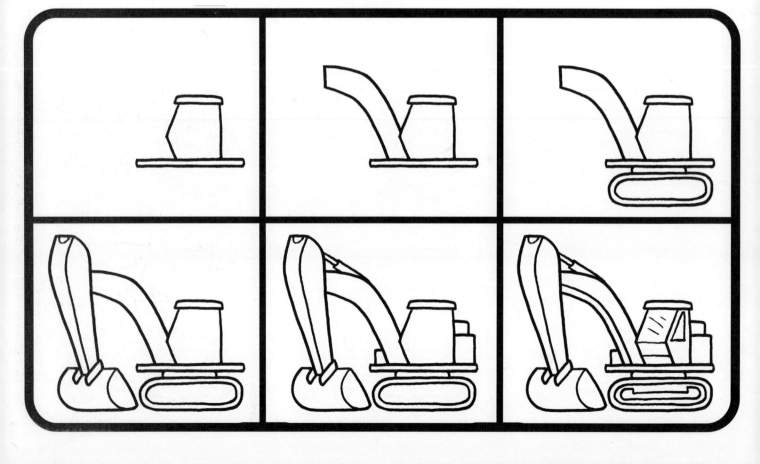

Lifeboat

Helicopter

Snowmobile

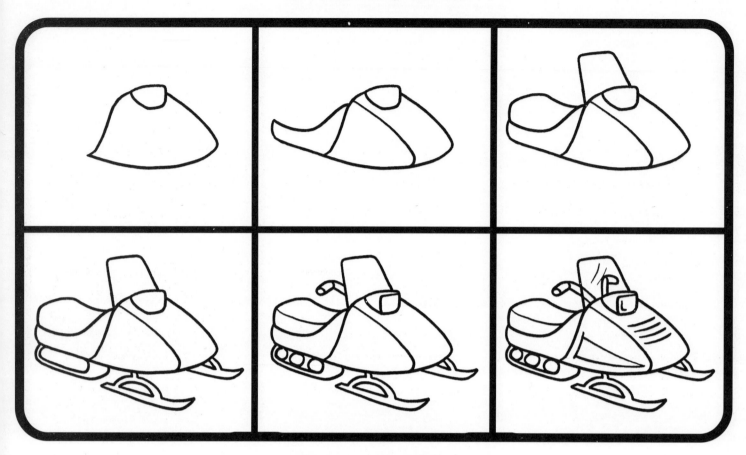

Moon Buggy

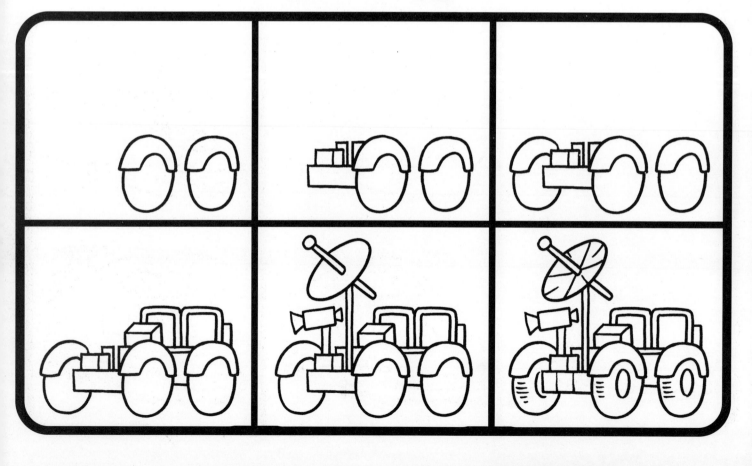

Crane

High Speed Train

Combine Harvester

Racing Motorbike

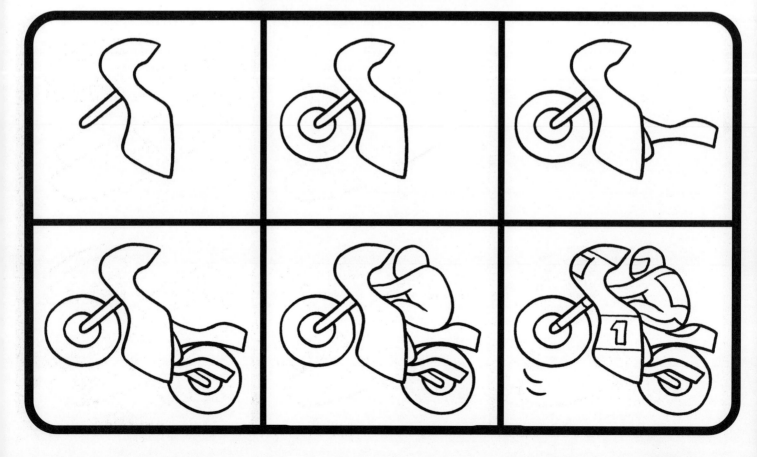

Police car

Wright Brothers' Flyer

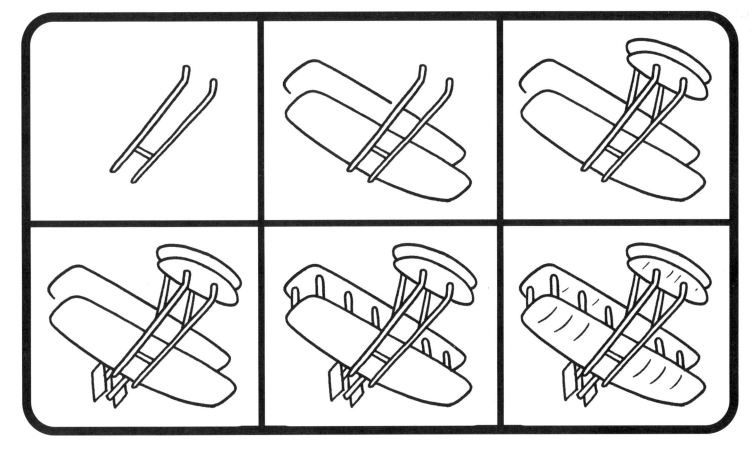

Mini Digger

Jet Ski

Space Shuttle

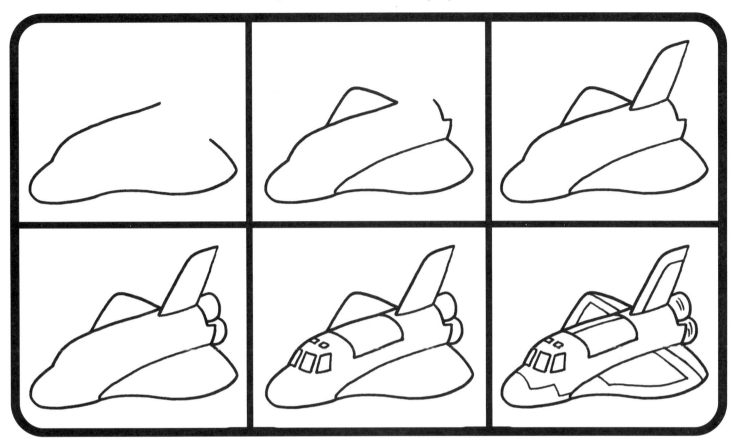

Chinese Junk Ship

Land Rover

Bullet Train

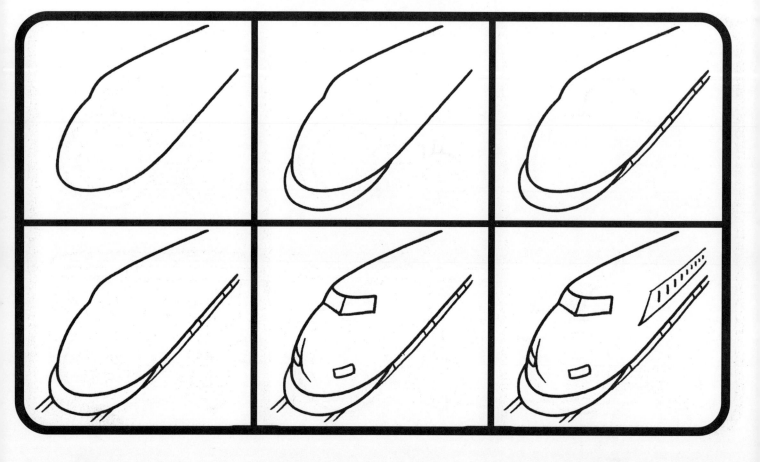

Motocross Bike

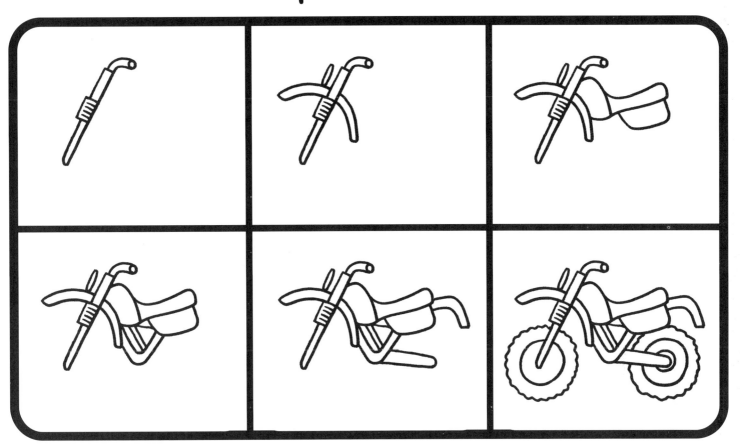

Traction Engine

Stealth fighter

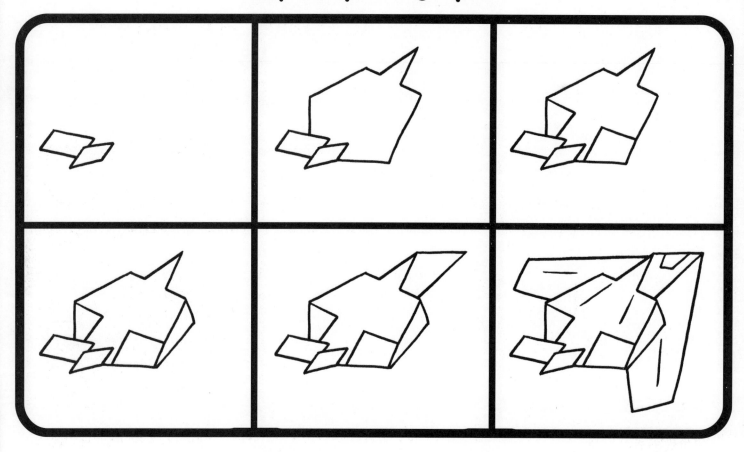

The first car

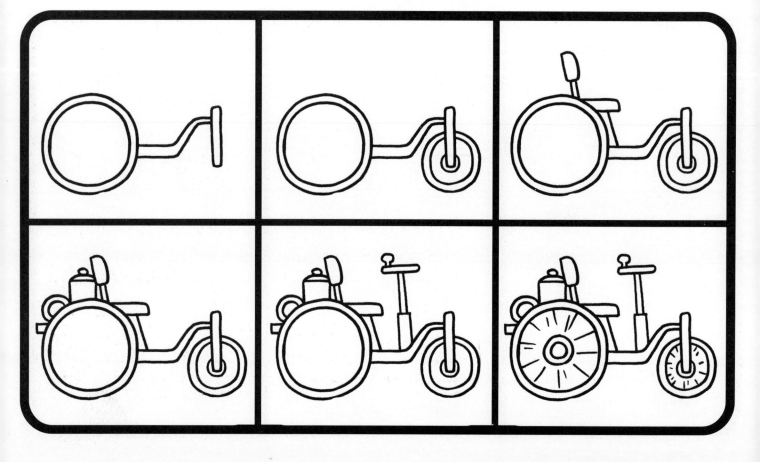

Dumper

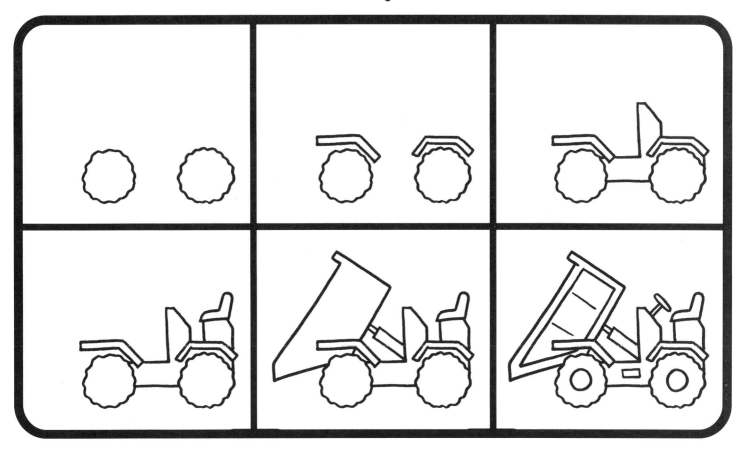

Cadillac

Motorized Rickshaw

Hydrofoil

Snow Plow Engine

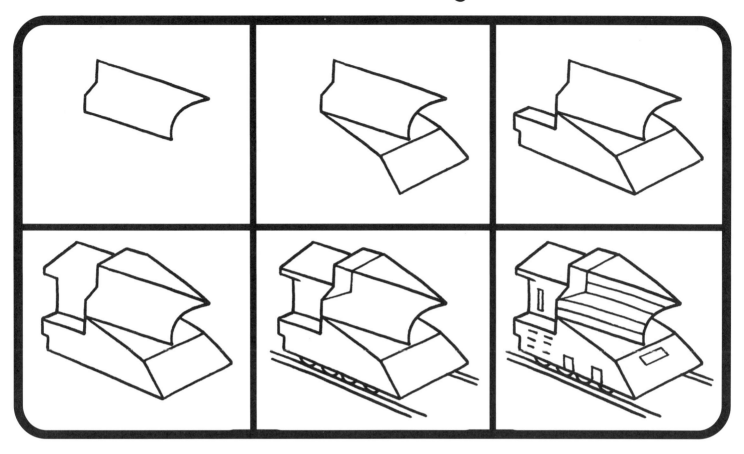

Spitfire

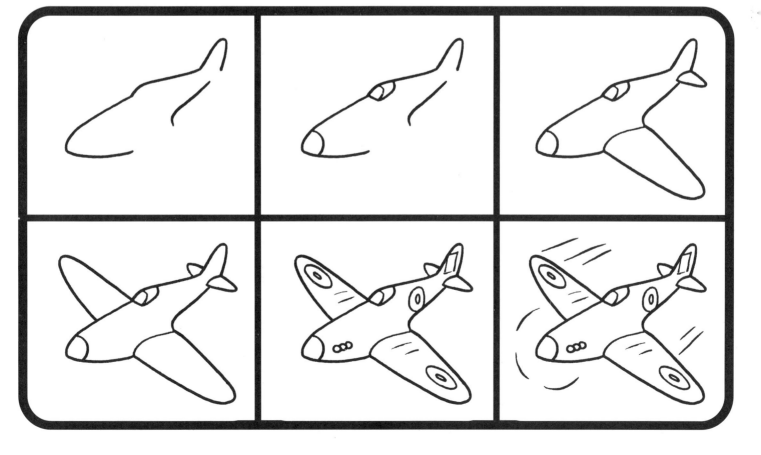

Bubble car

cement Truck

Ultralight

Paddle Steamer

17th Century Ship

Monster Truck

Dumper Truck

Scooter

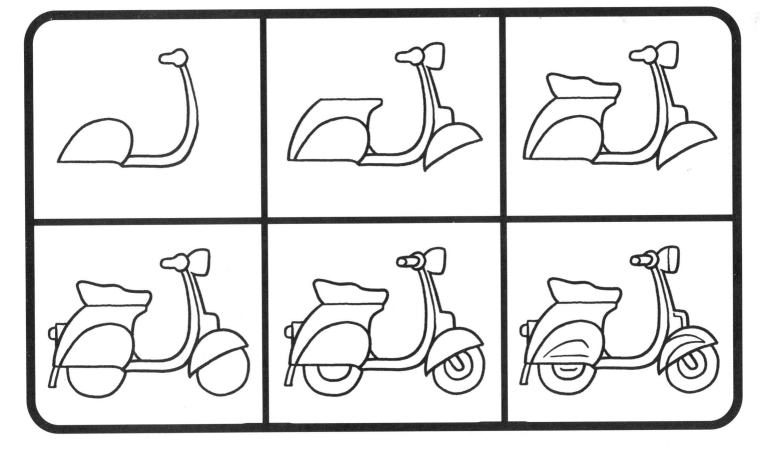

Le Mans Racing car

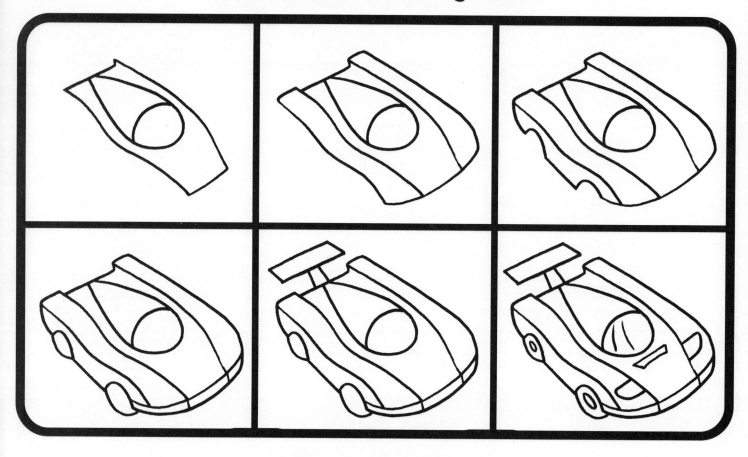

Skip Truck

Hovercraft

The Mallard Train

Roller

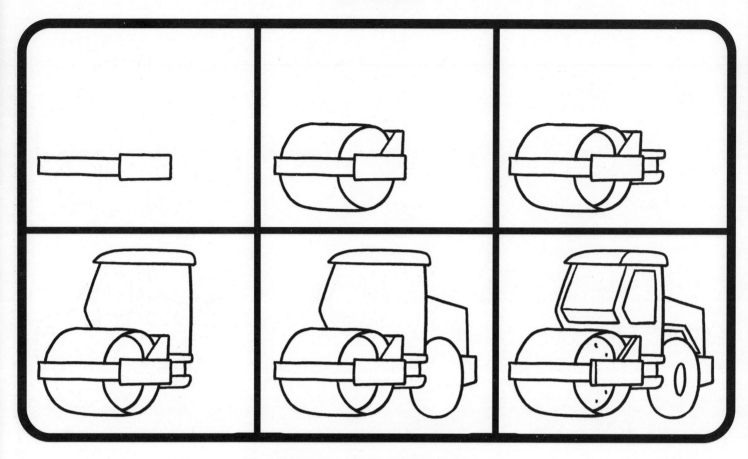

Fishing Boat

Pickup Truck

Lorry

Speed Boat

1901 oldsmobile

Seaplane

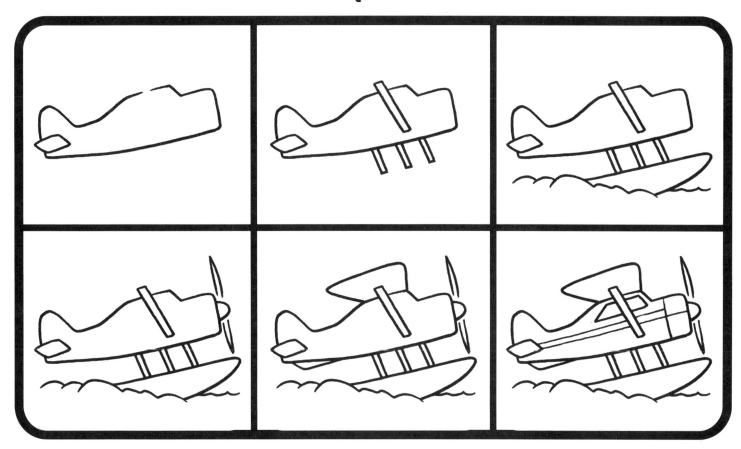

London Bus

Tractor

Snow cat

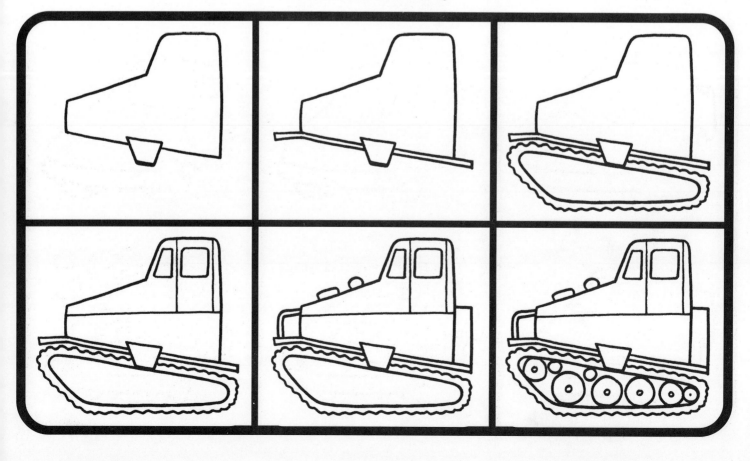

Fire Engine

Stock car

Thrust II

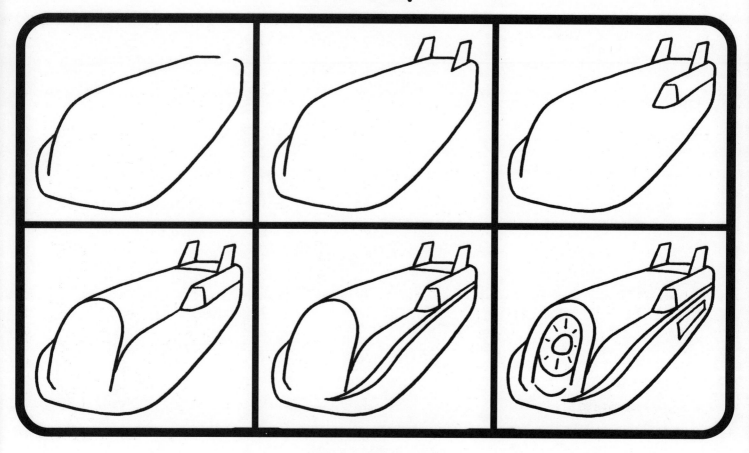

Tug Boat

The Rocket

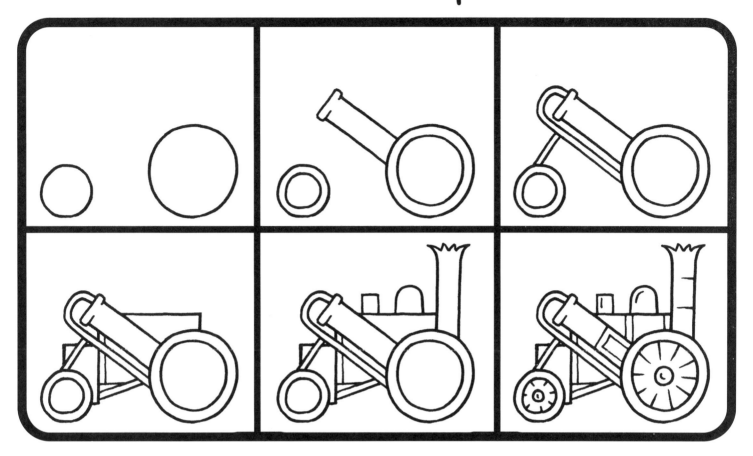

Citroen 2CV

Quad Bike

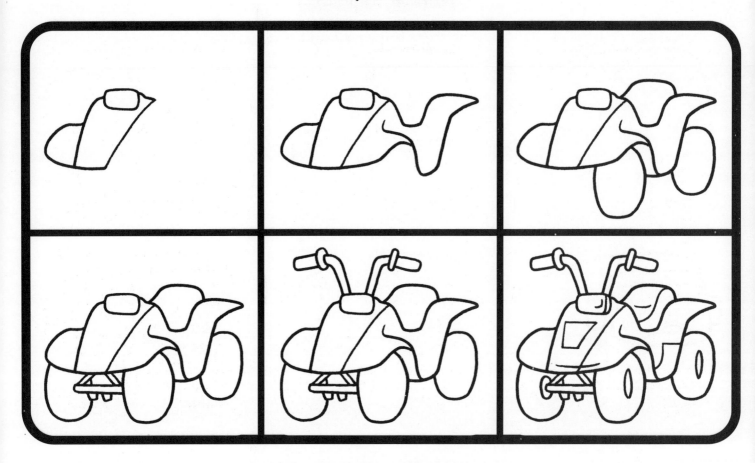

London Taxi

Bus

Submersible

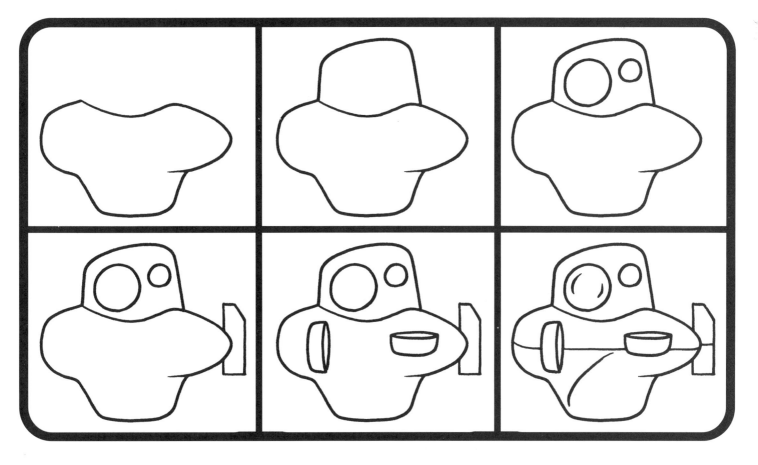

1920s Motorbike

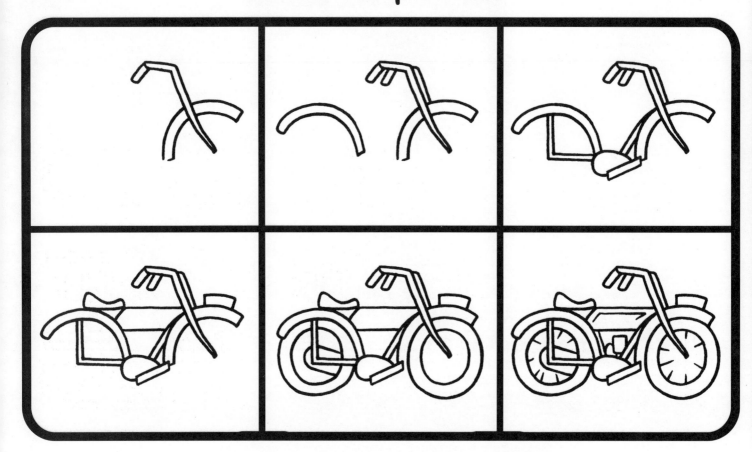

Concept Electric Car

Bulldozer

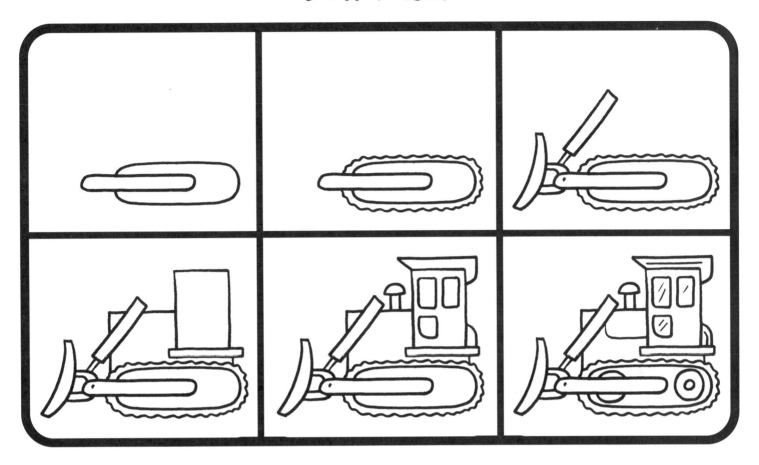

4x4 Off-Road Vehicle

Rolls Royce

Light Aircraft

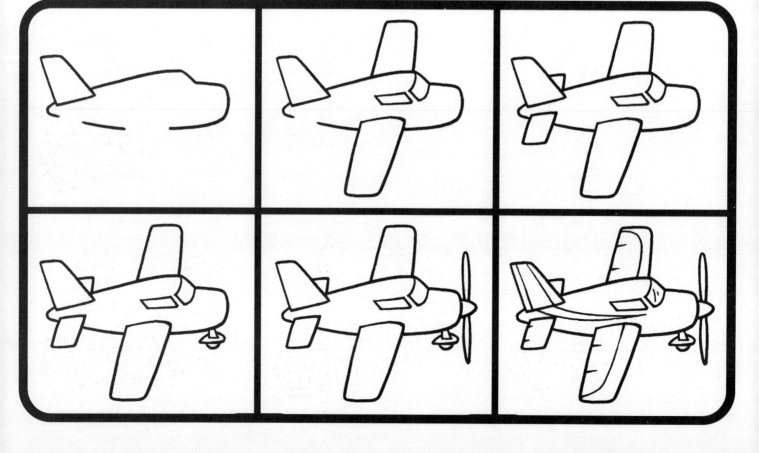

Dragster

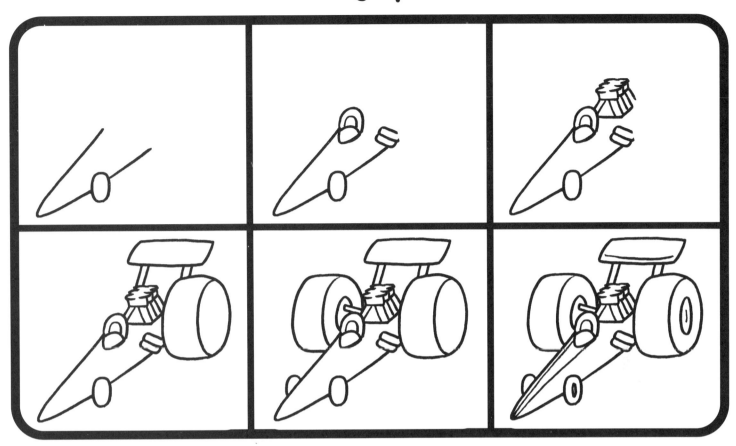

Wild West Train

Model T ford

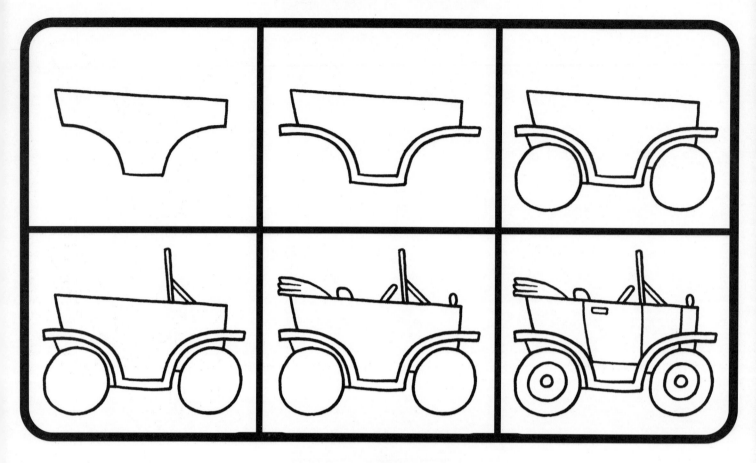

Dune Buggy

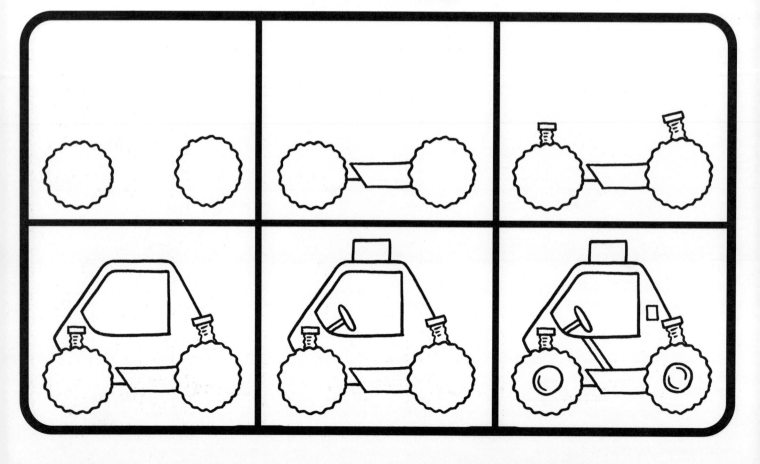

Gossamer Albatross

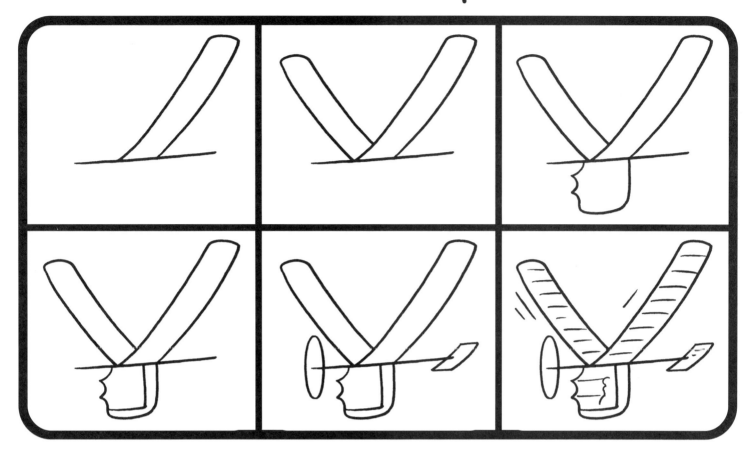

Forklift Truck

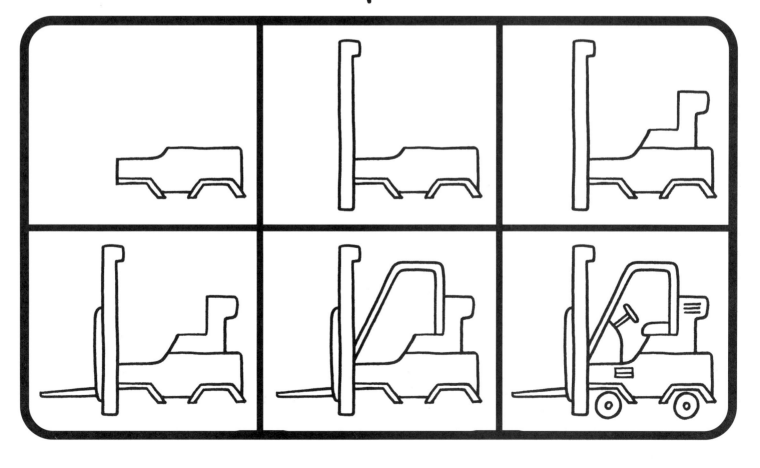

concorde

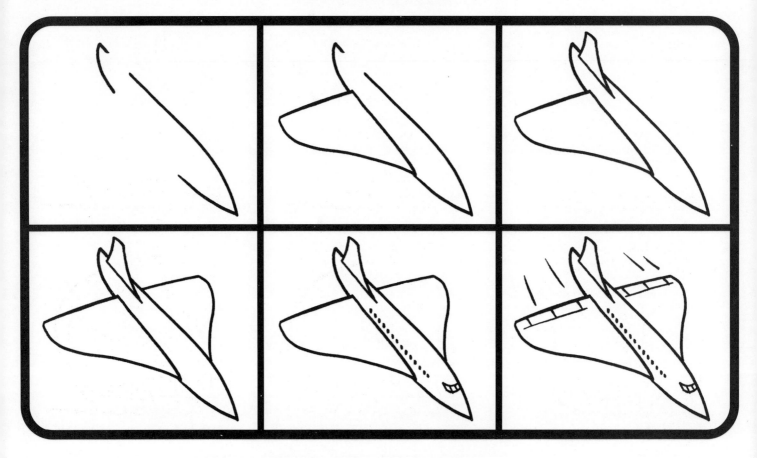

Stretch Limo

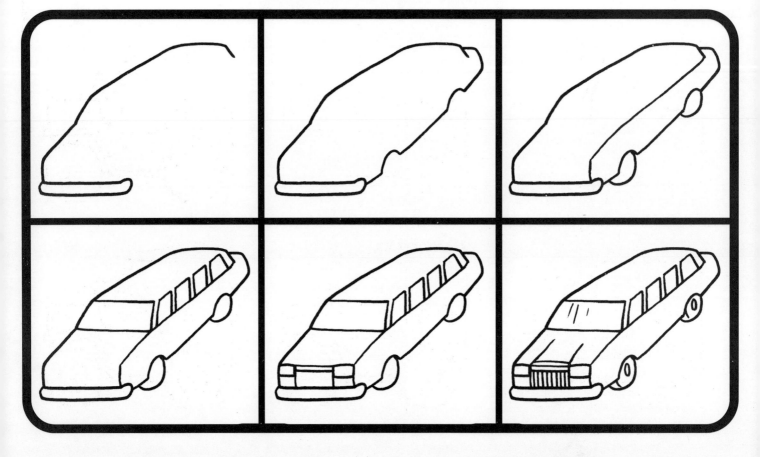

Yacht

Jeep

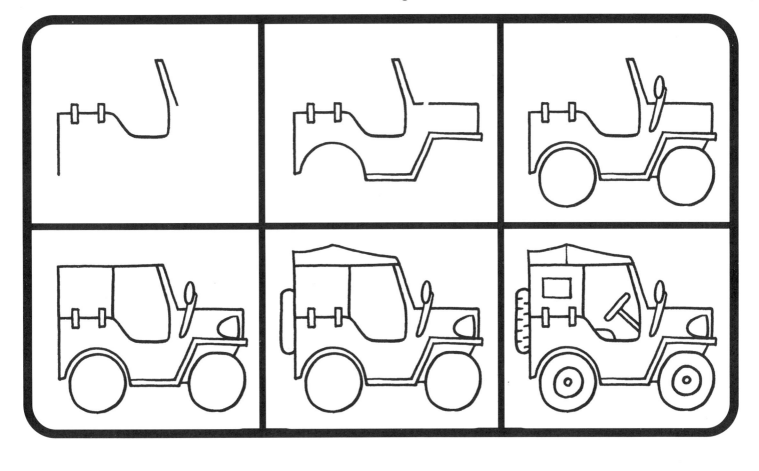

Submarine

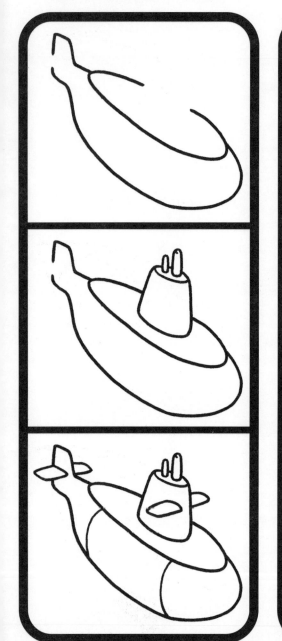

Biplane

Monorail Train

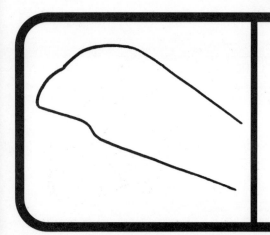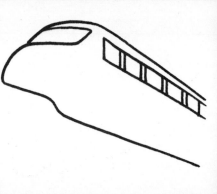

cable car

Sunray

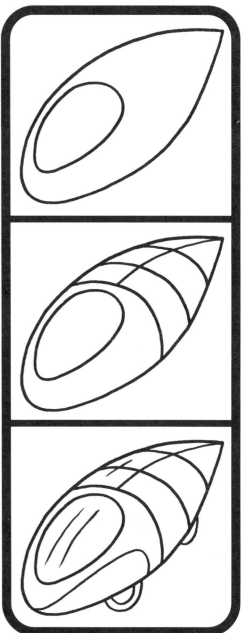

Airship

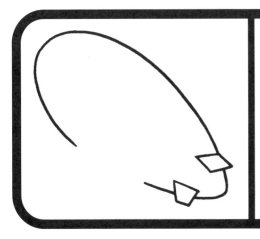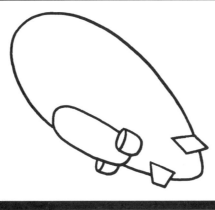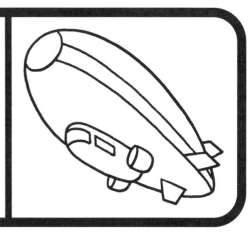

VW Beetle

Van

Hang-glider

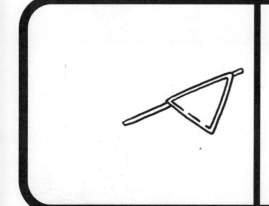

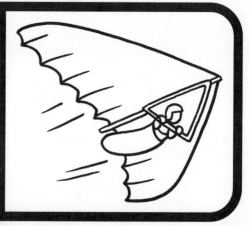

funicular

Rocket

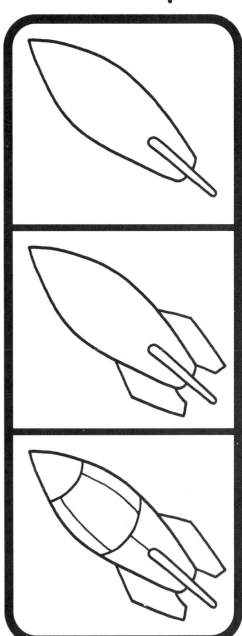

Lindbergh's "Spirit of St. Louis"

Glider

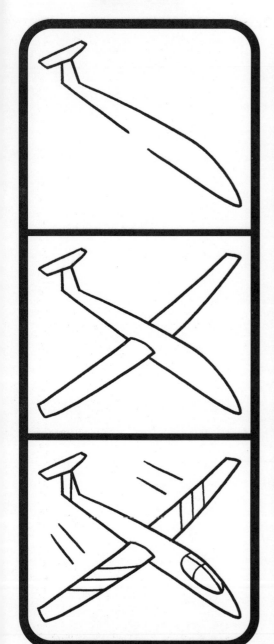

Tram

Bell X-1 Rocket

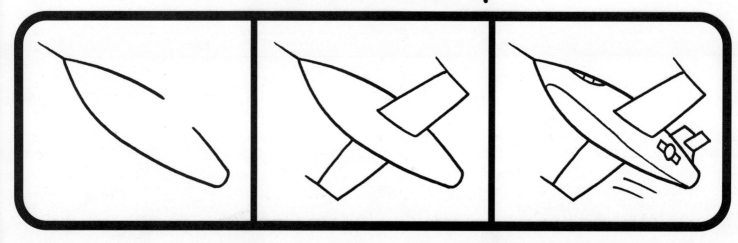

Ponytail

Young Girl

Teddy cuddle

Happy Girl

School Girl

Trendy Girl

catsuit

Skipping

Dancing   # Cool Girl

Sleepyhead

Curly Hair

Thumbs Up

Annoyed

Laid Back   Shy Girl

Braids

School Boy

Soccer Player   Angry Boy

Grumpy Boy

Relaxed

Trendy Boy

Cool Boy

Smart Boy　　Waving

cookies   # yo-yo

Attitude

Skater

Shy Boy

Bandana

Hoody

Ready to Go

Magical Woman

Business Woman

Dancer

Athletic Woman

Racer

Walker

Karate Girl

Japanese Lady

Psychic

Winter Woman

Mother

Archer

Smart Lady

Party Woman

Smart Guy

Relaxed Dude

Karate

Runner

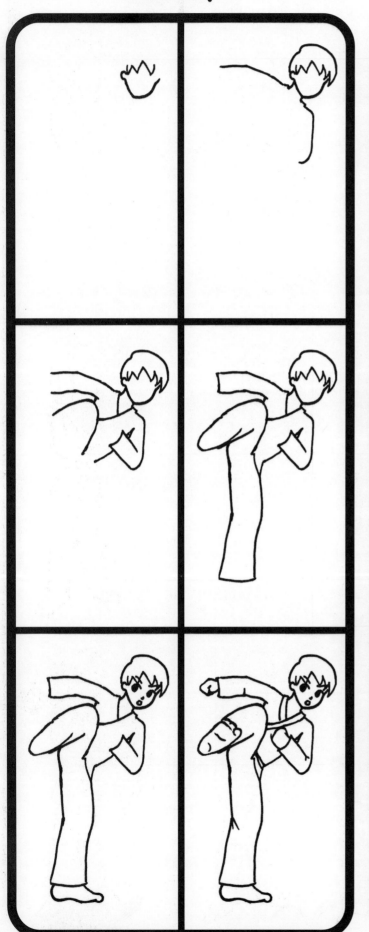

Arms Folded

Elf Archer

Spaceman

Magician

Mystic

Aviator

Rocker

cool Man

Leader

cool Dude

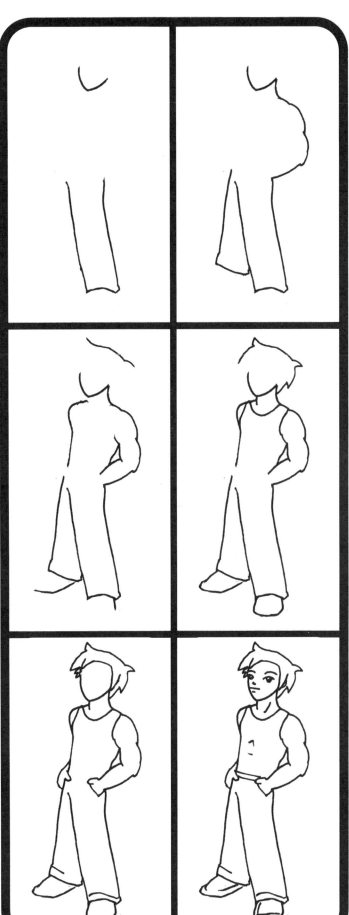

Lamsa

Firefoxy

Shetlan

Springfoot

Anloo

Groob

Bim

Floopsey

Fire Storm

Mewm

Frosty

Twitch

Anglor

Flambow

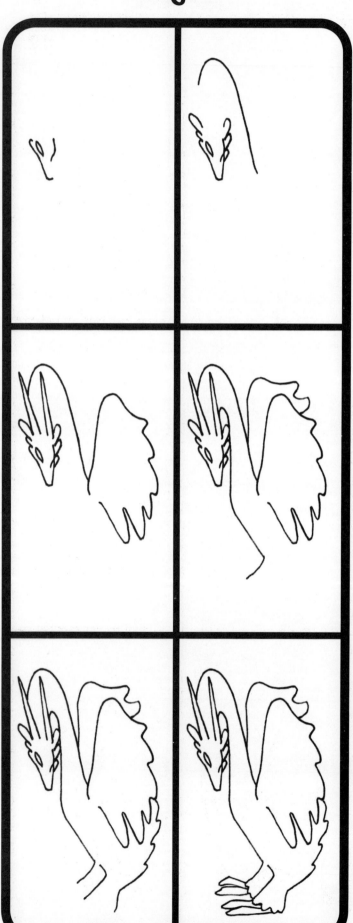

Jelojoup

Brushtail

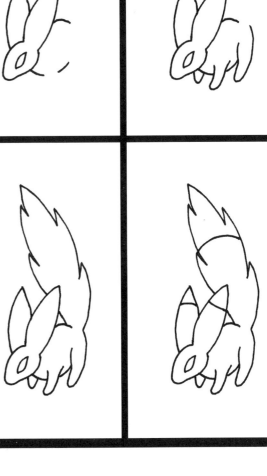

Robot 1   # Robot 2

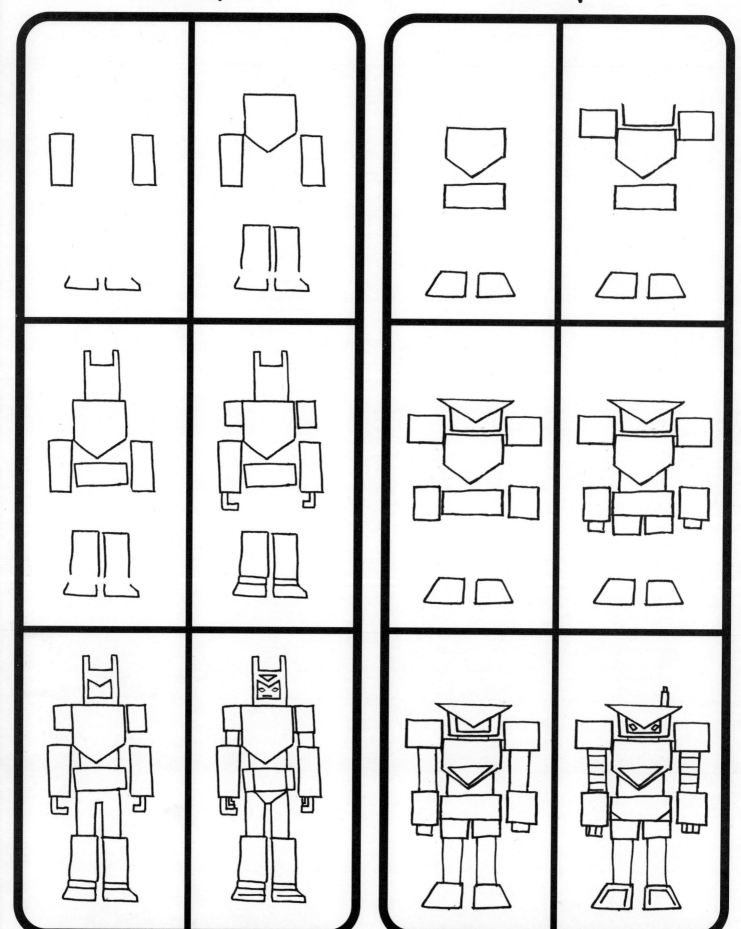

Robot 3

Robot 4

Robot 5

Robot 6

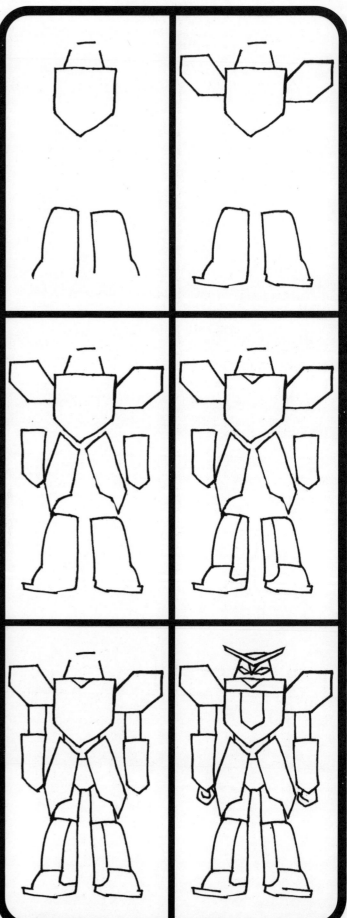

Robot 7

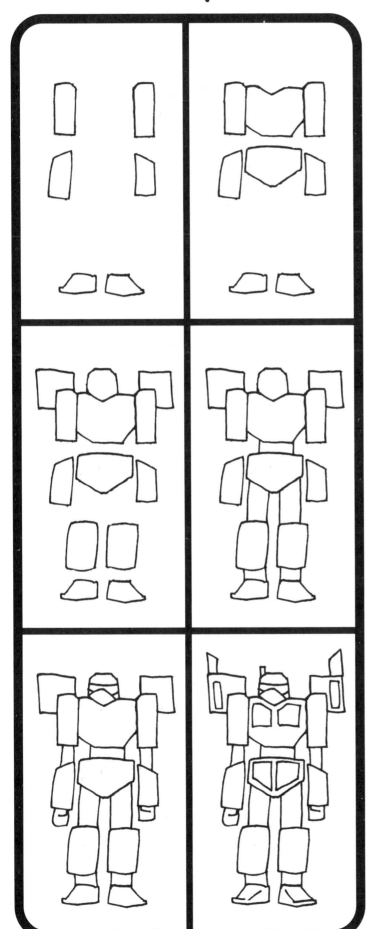

Robot 8

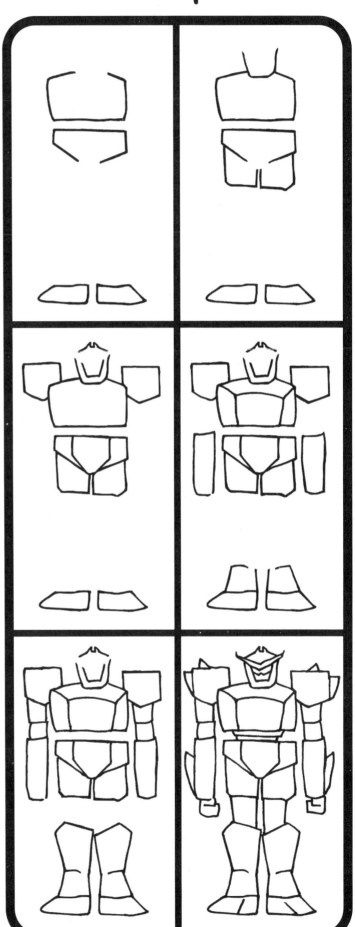

Pleased

Interested

Shy

Happy

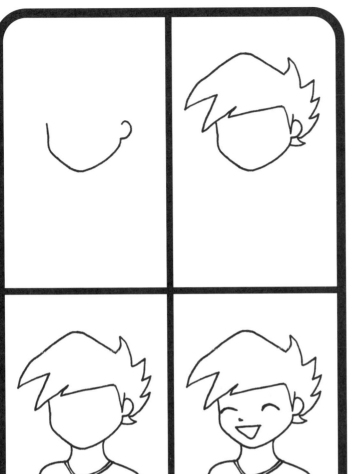

Amazed

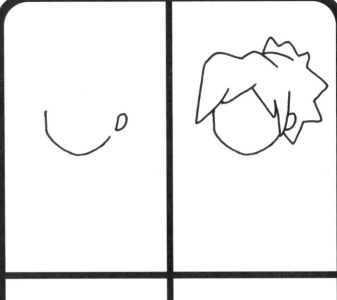

Worried

cross

Crying

Shouting

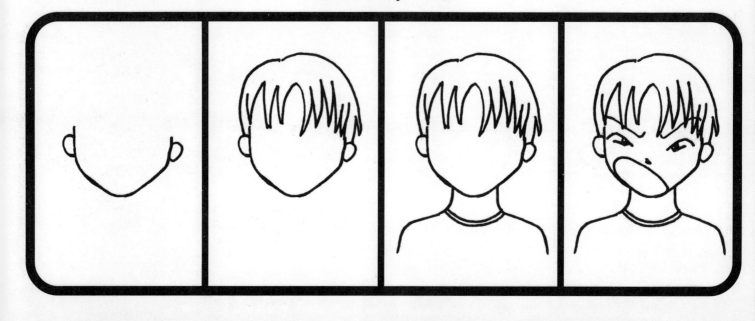

Shock

Wink

Tongue out

Fed Up

Demure

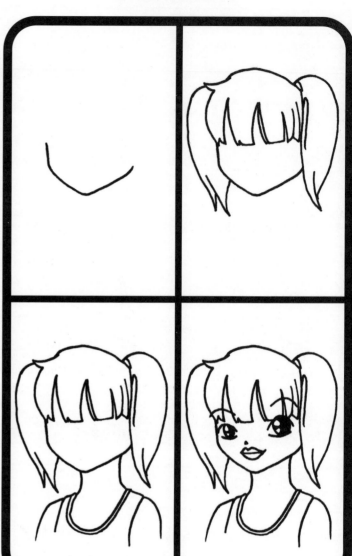

Thinking

Snozz

Gargoyle

Snorky

Gumph

Jarred

crab

Nessie

Matilda

Eyeball

Sloppy

Trog   Hairy

Slither   # Hag

Bull

Snout

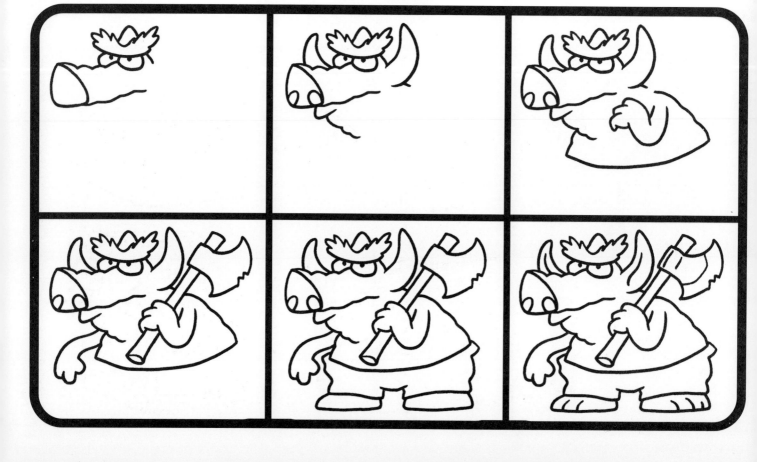

Rough

Troll-In-The-Box

Batty

Snurkle

Mertle

Spider

Shaggy

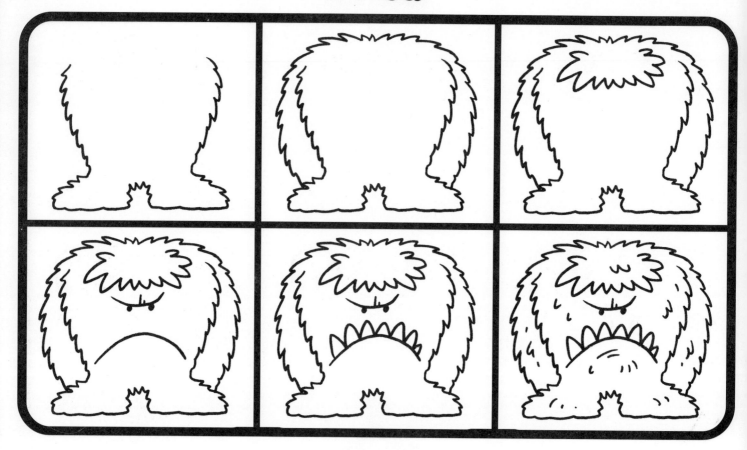

Wavy

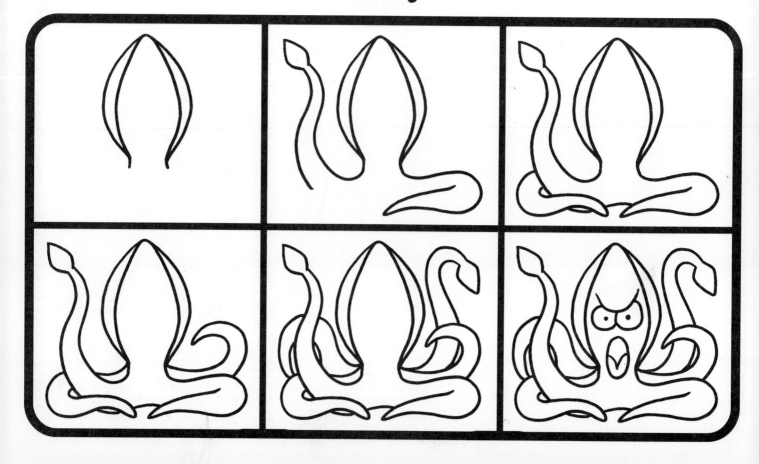

Pet

Vampire

Rah

Blob

Dev

Rock

Slimey

Slug

Flokk

Gumble

Warty

Dragon

Ted

Smelly

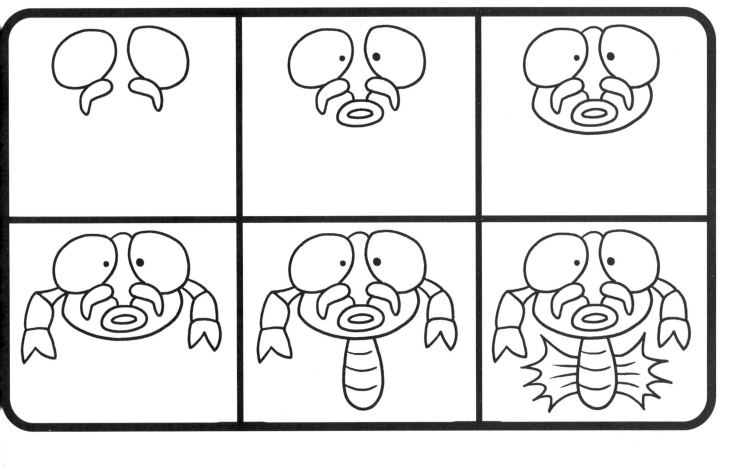

colly

cloaked

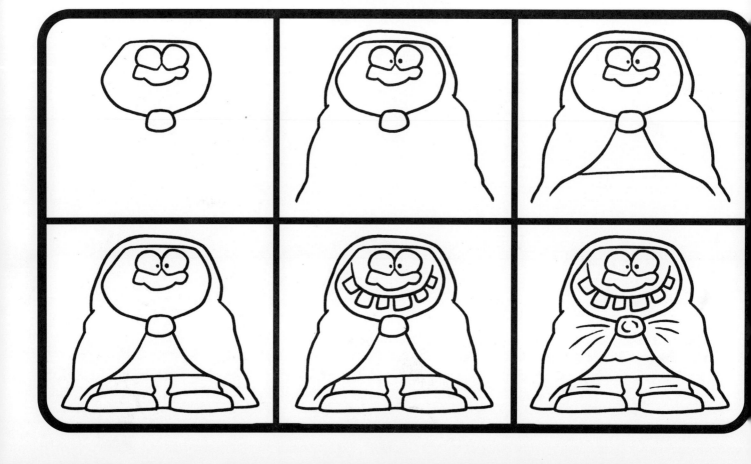

Sharky

Larry

Potty

Verm

Horn

Tree

Stocky

Mummy

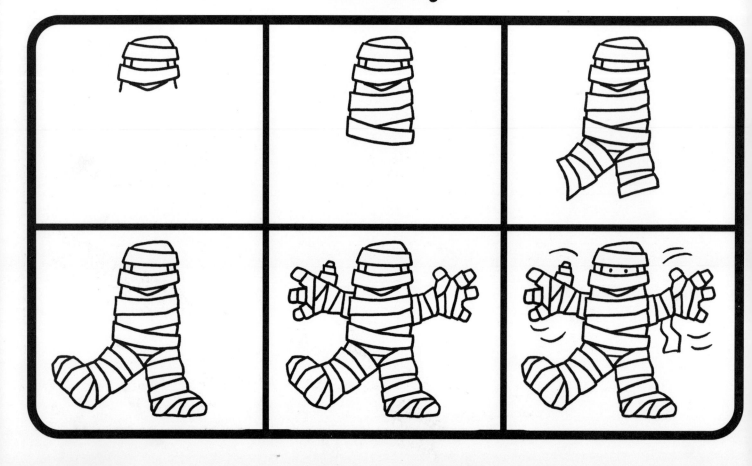

Big one

Bendy

Eavesdrop

Squabble

Skull

Snail

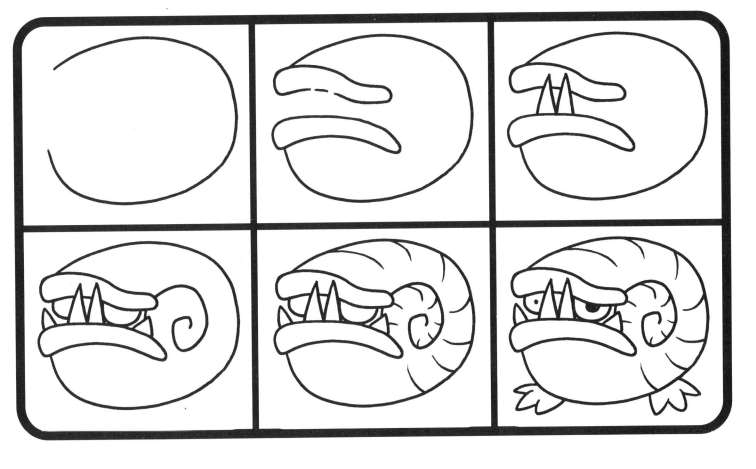

Rambo

Gloom

cyclops

Glum

Scary

Medusa

Jagged

Aaargh!

Troll

Bert

Hal

Nerd

Phantom

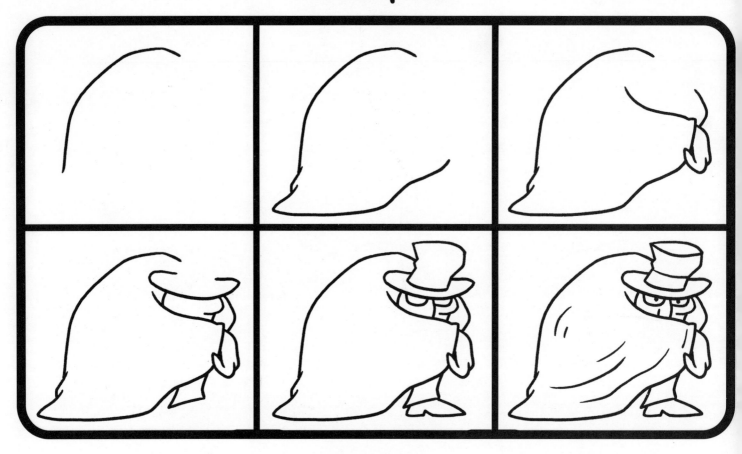

Squat

Werewolf

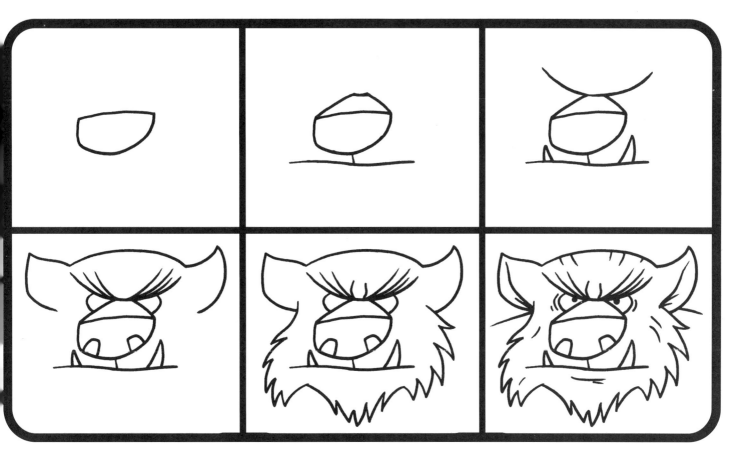

Robot

Lippy   Merlin

Gran

Gramps

Fingers

Pumpkin

Spot

Triton

Baby

Happy

Growl

Wingding

Google   # Johnny

Exterminate

Vanilla

Hattie

Bulldog

Venus flytrap

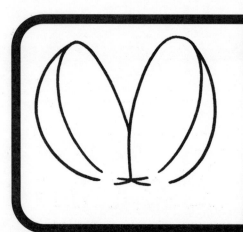 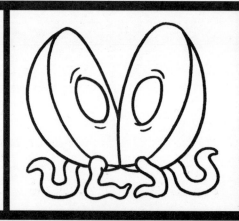 

Slurp

Horned Beast

Big Mouth

Snorkel

Helmet

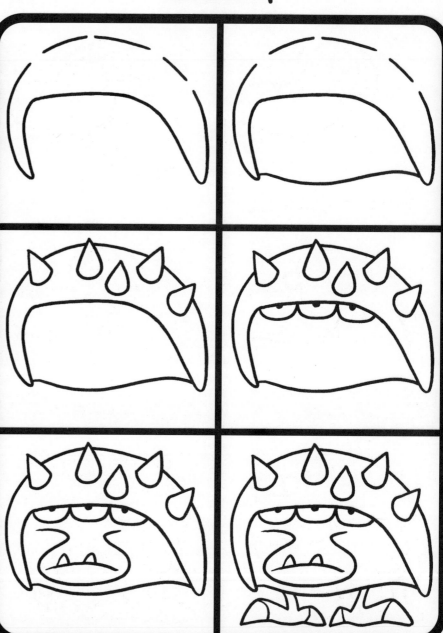

Herm

Beaky

Woo

Slump

Goggle Eyes

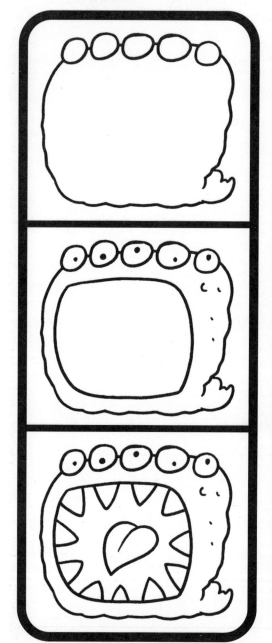

Truck

Slime

Snakehead   # Super Sleuth

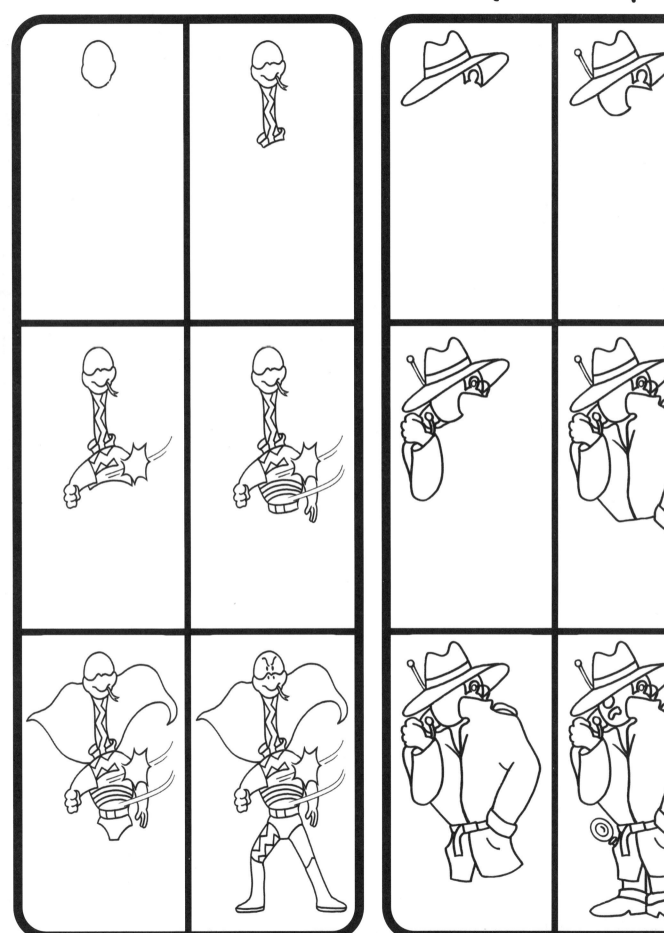

Star Pilot

Super Bug

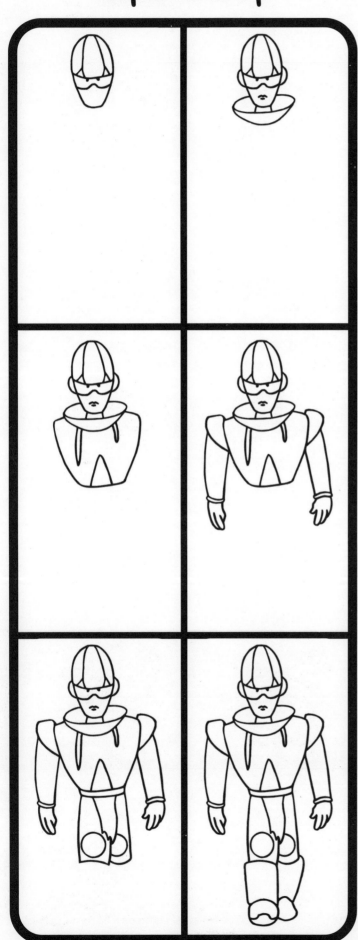

Super Gloo

Princess Mighty

Super Lady   Jaws

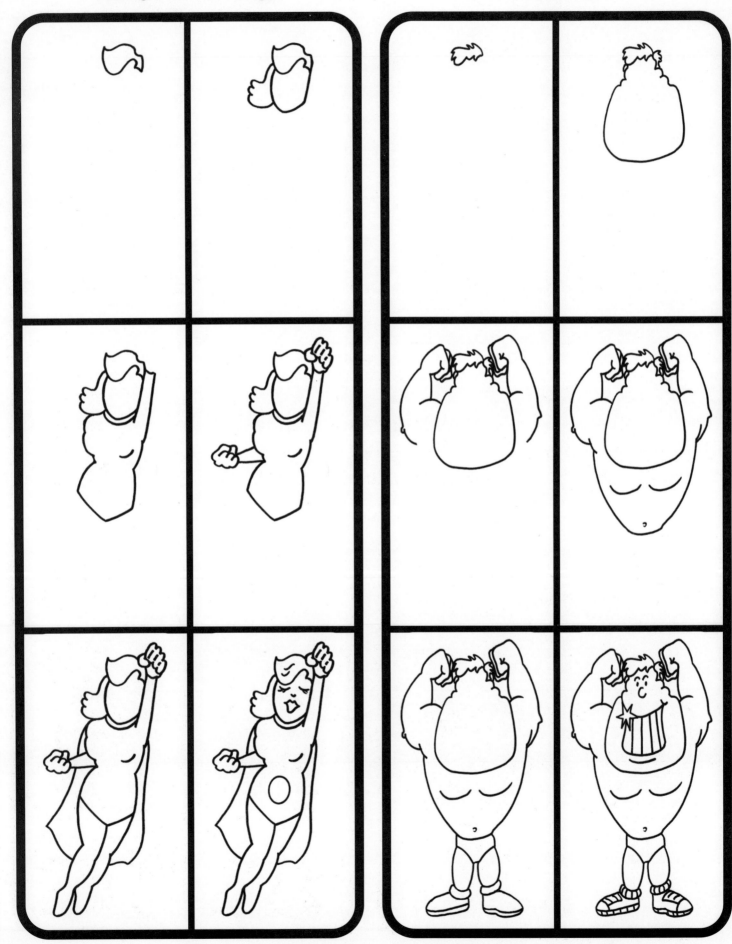

Super Thor   Super caveman

Blade Warrior

Celtic Warrior

Super Mom   # Jungle Man

Robin Hood

Dragon Queen

Sir-Lance-A-Lot

Hannibal

Super Duck

Hammer Head

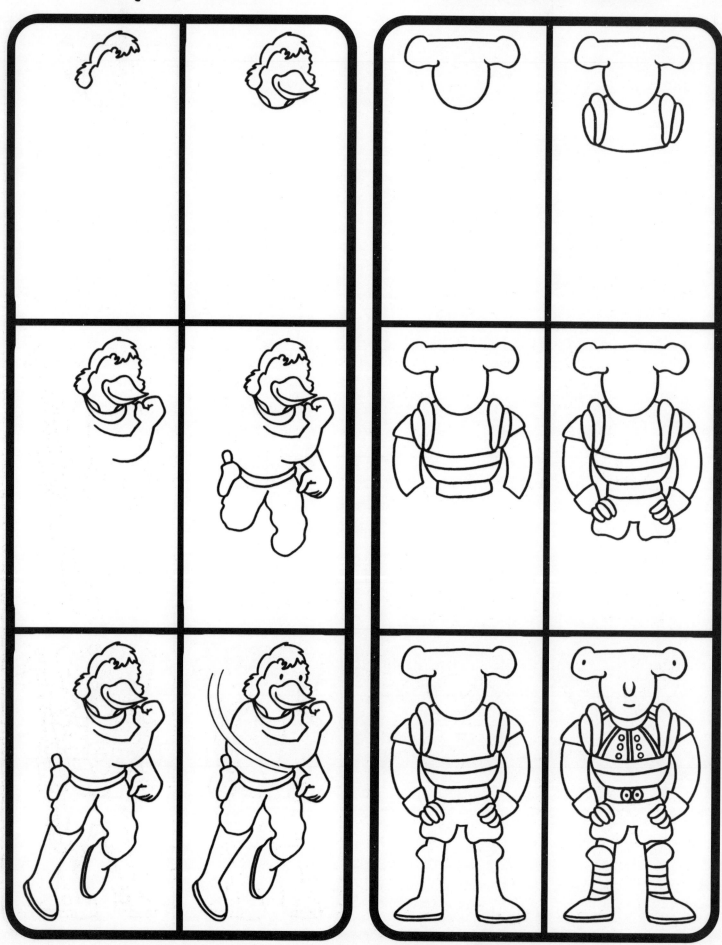

Super Moose

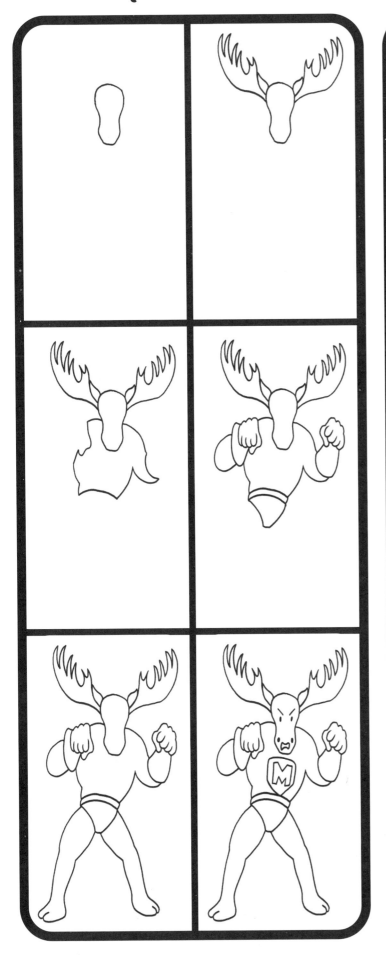

Volgan

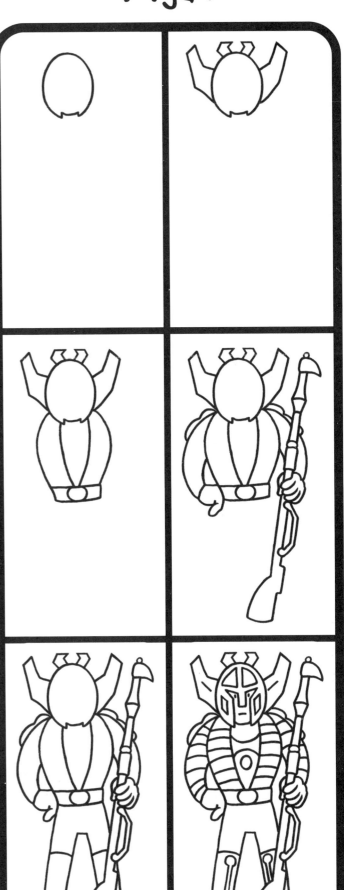

Buffalo Bill

Galactica

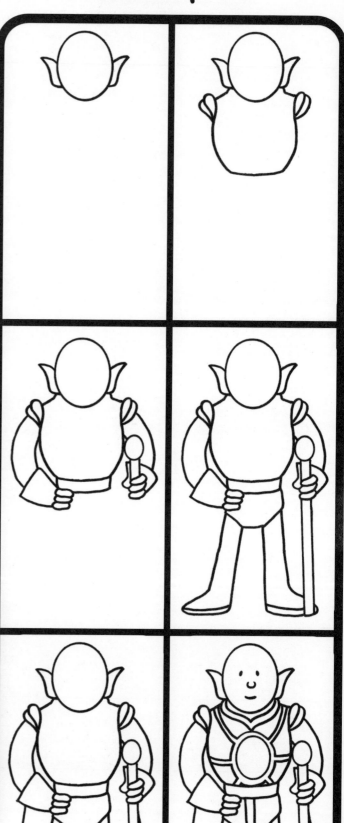

Super oil

Rope Breaker

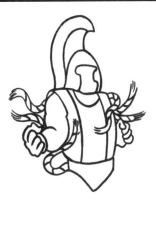

The Bat

Globe Man

Space Robot

Space Baroness

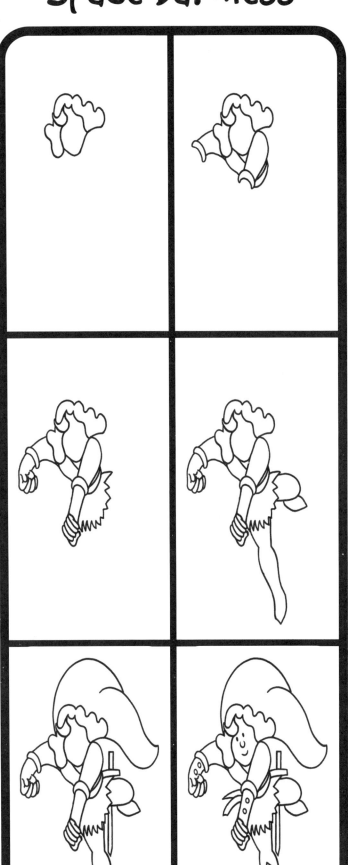

Space Warrior

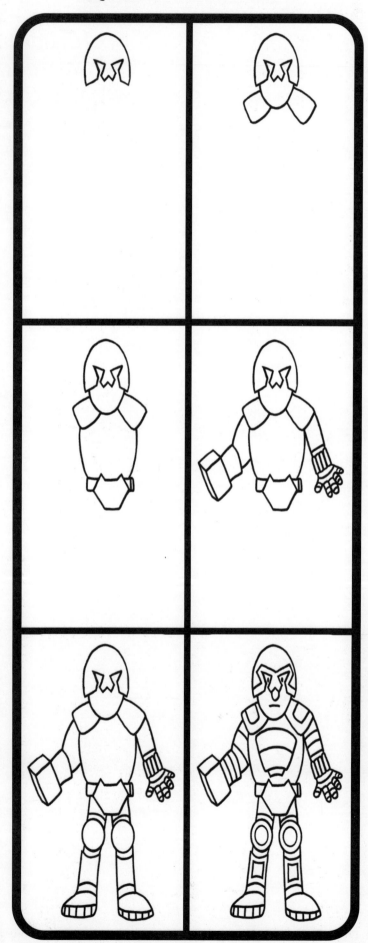

Sonic Hero

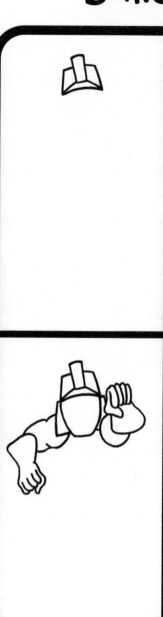

Mechanic Man

Demon Fighter

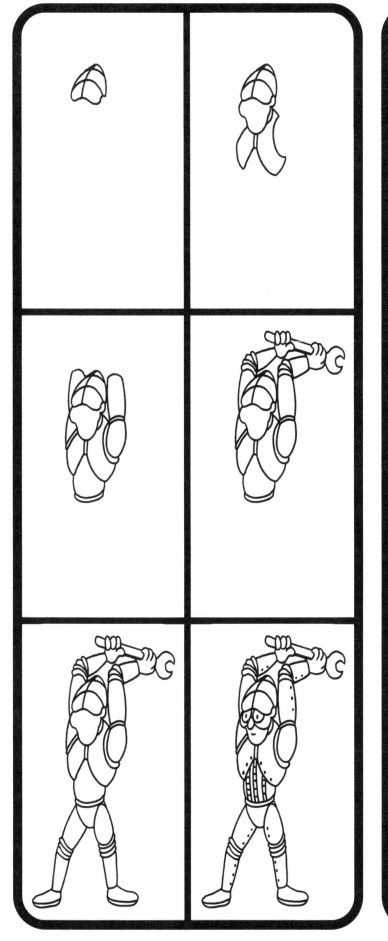

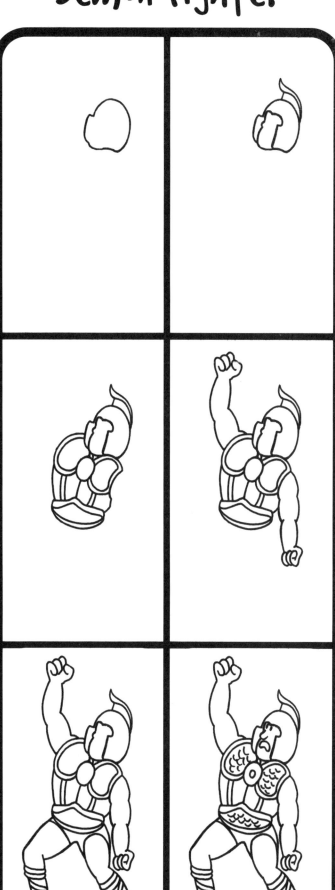

Demon Slayer   Lightning Diver

UDDz

Captain Galactic

Ninja

Axeman

The Archer   # Lightning

Sky Boxer

Venus Amazon

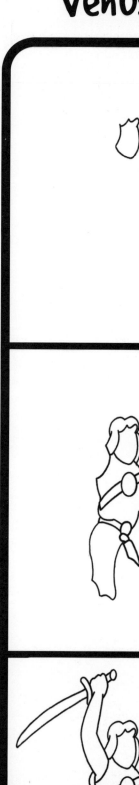

Star Warden

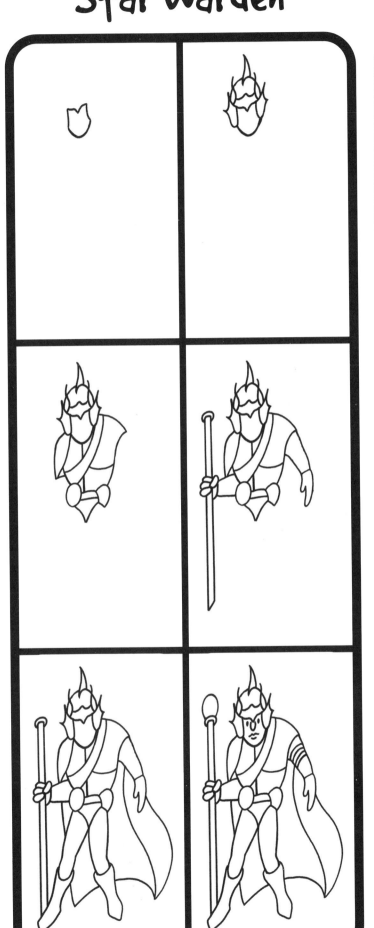

Spartacus

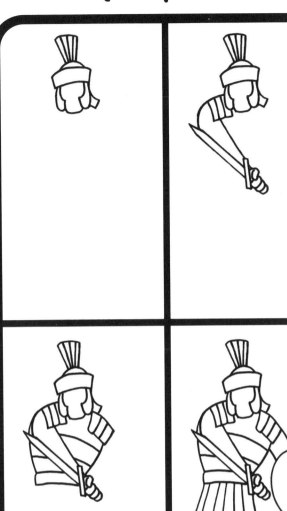

Star Hunter   # Space Shield

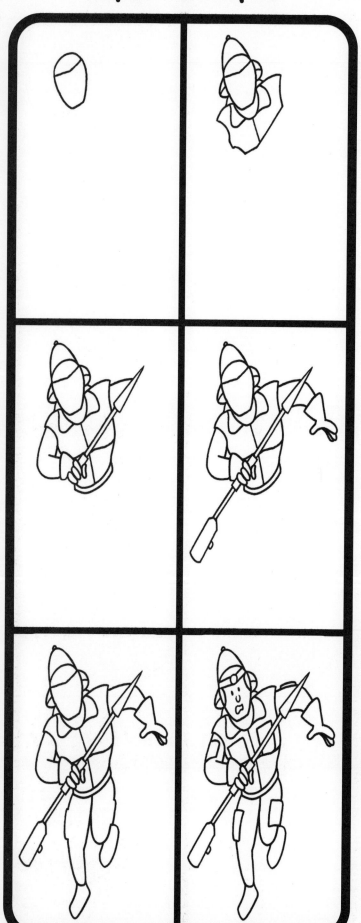

Kajo

Zulu

Robot Warrior

Frogman

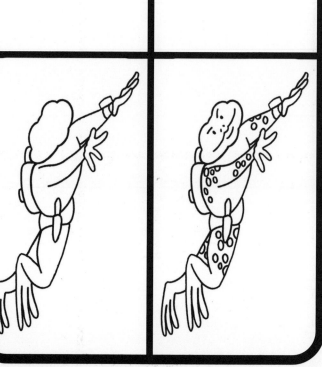

Space Sniper

Prince Sword

Karate King

Sky Diver

Super Saver

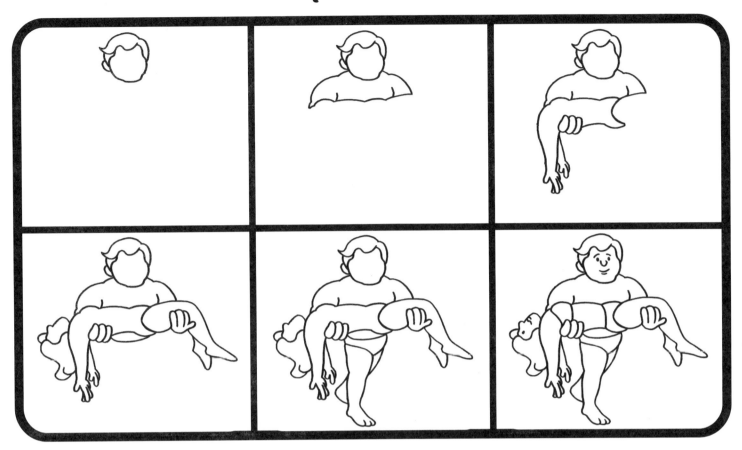

Samurai

Queen Boudicca

Aztec

Super Star

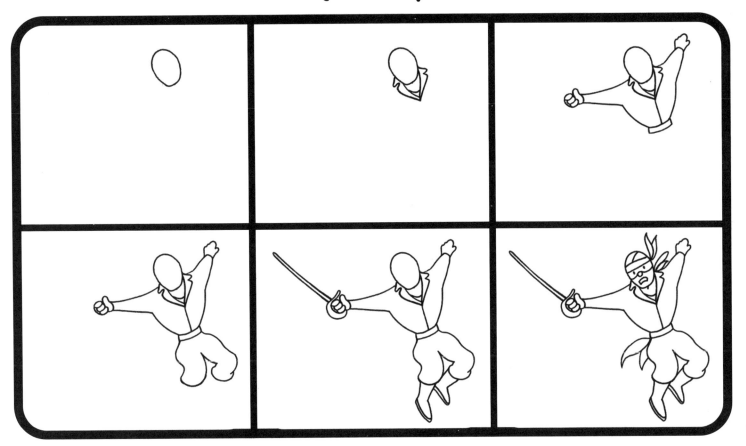

Sky Leaper

Swash Buccaneer

Space Skater

Lizardus

Surf Boarder

Super Egor

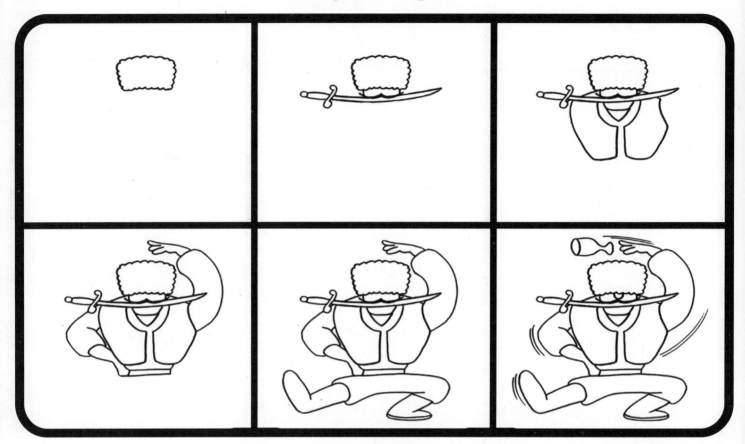

Skater

Space Queen

Super Charger

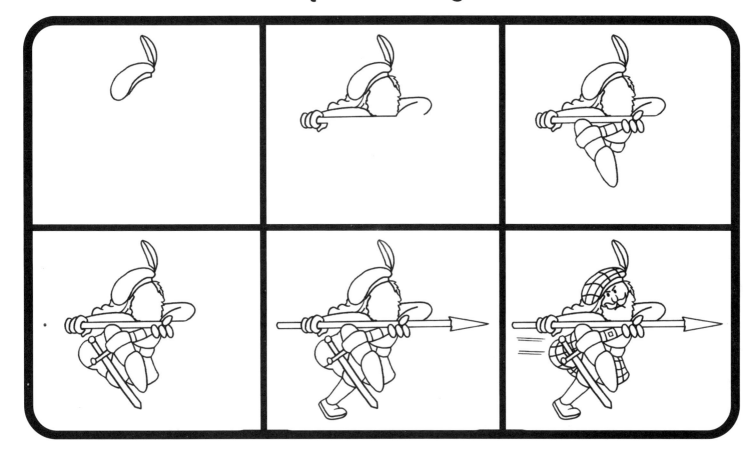

G.I.

Markovian Lancer

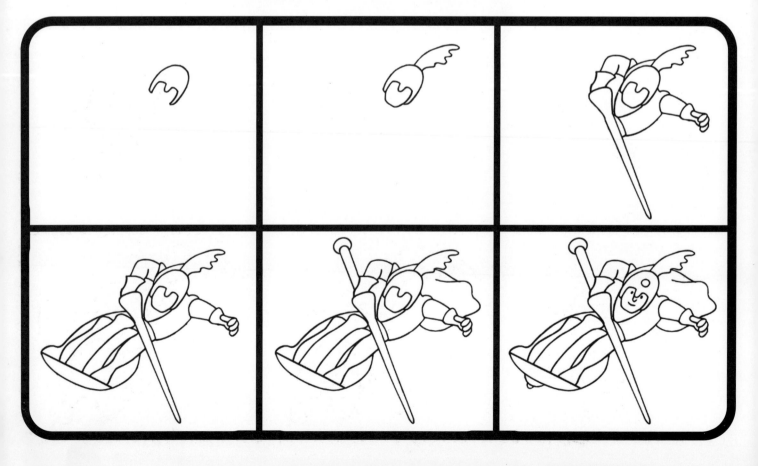

Greek Hero

Sky Scraper

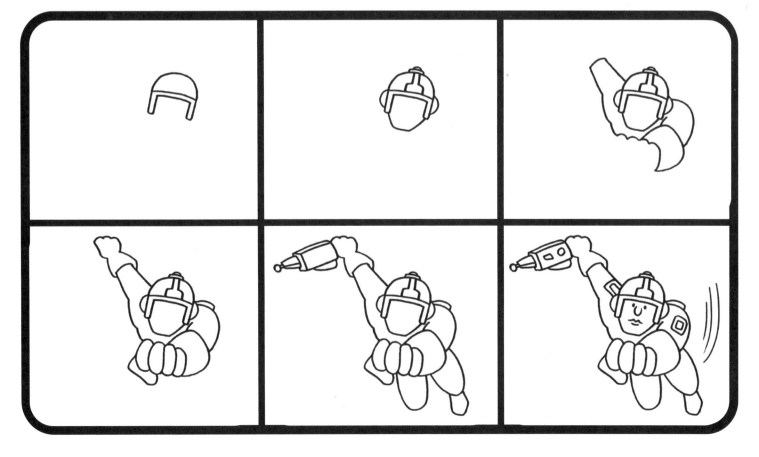

Robo

Kango Kicker

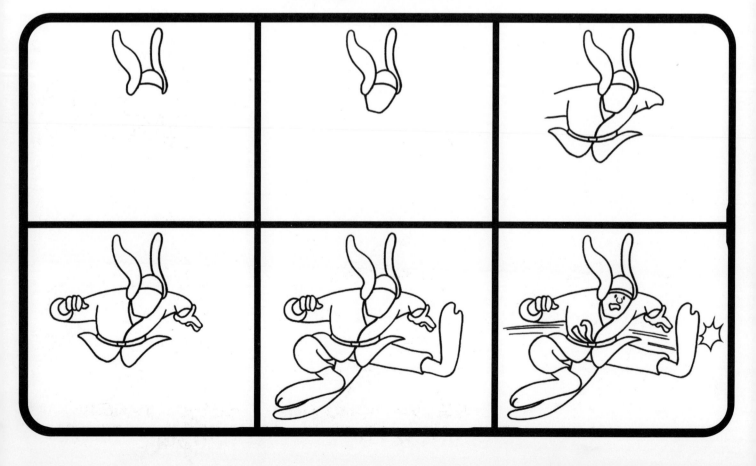

Star chaser

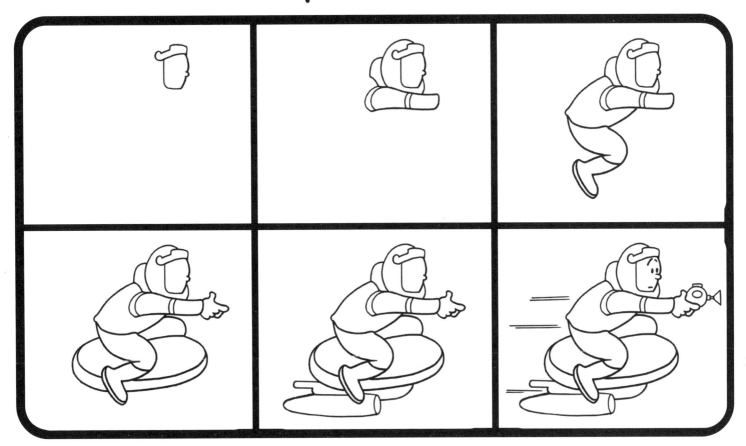

Rocky Hunter

Super Power

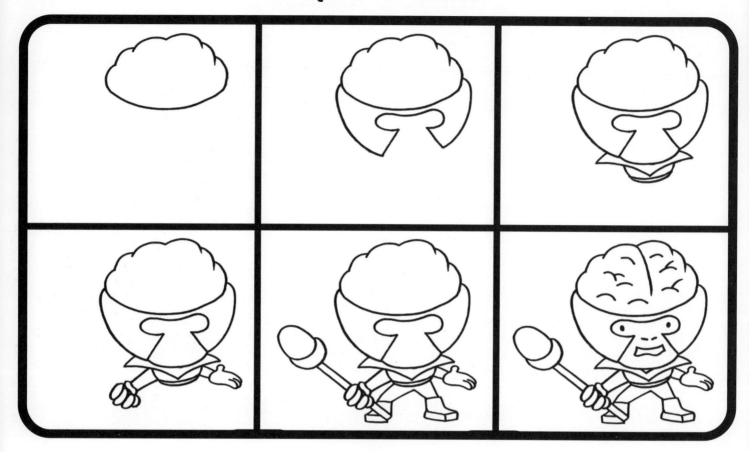

Android

Super Silly-us

Kongo

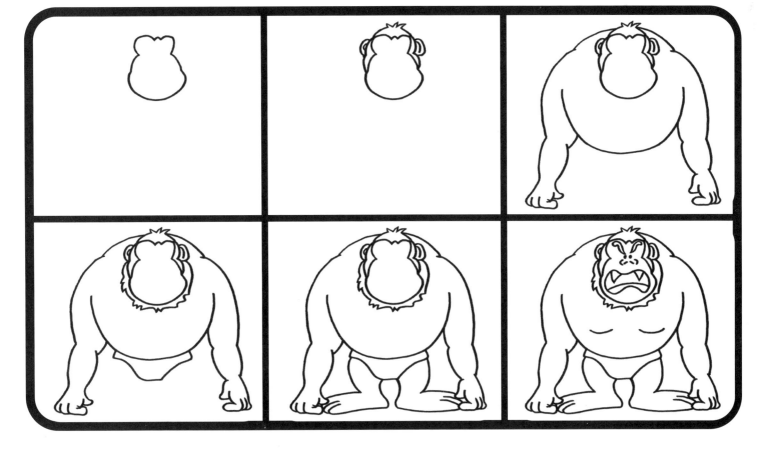

Star Skater

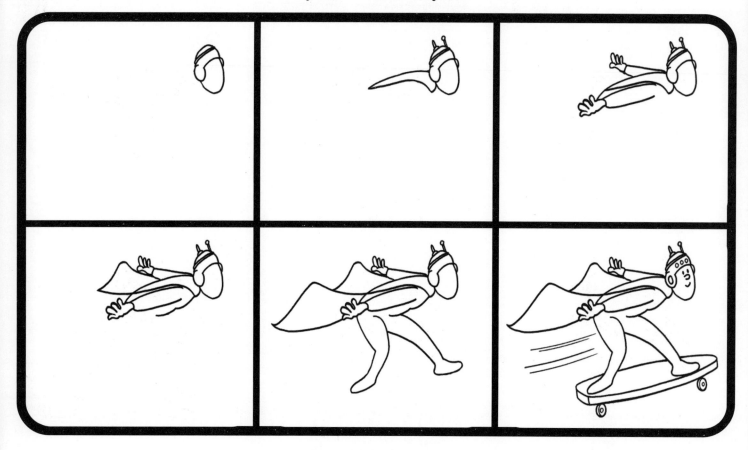

Arachnia

Layzar

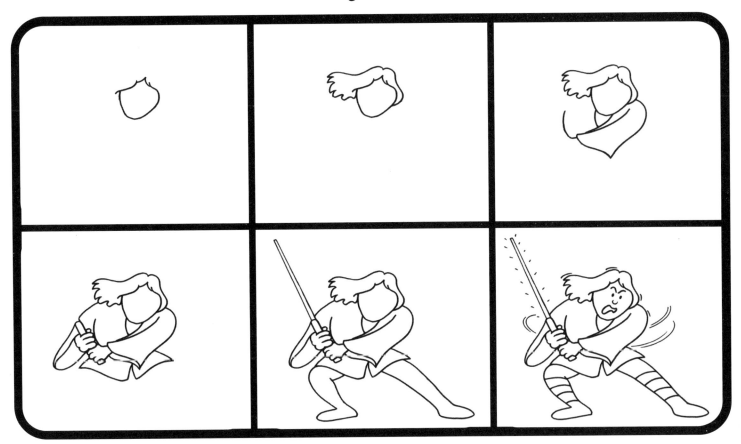

Super Swooper

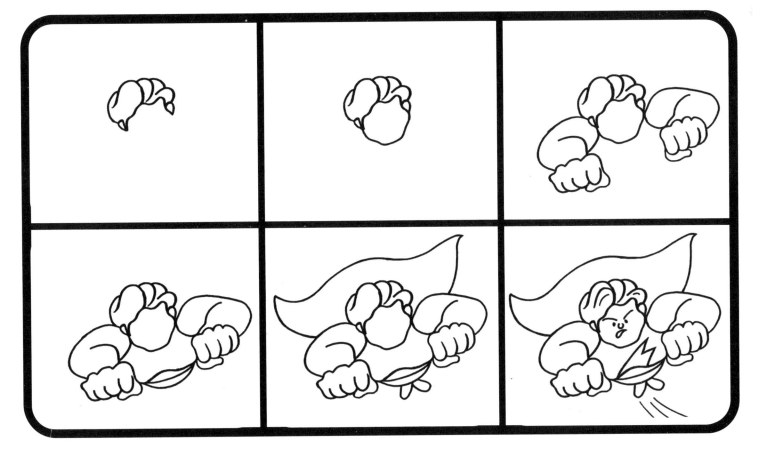

Super Nan

Barbarus

Super Flyer

Space Lancer

Super Spy

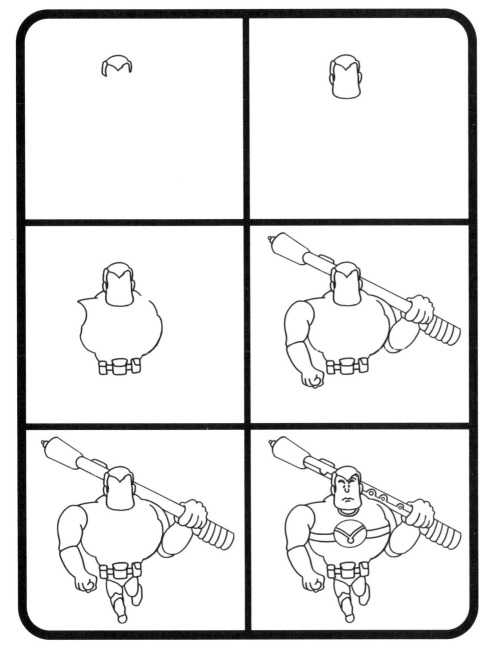

Goliath

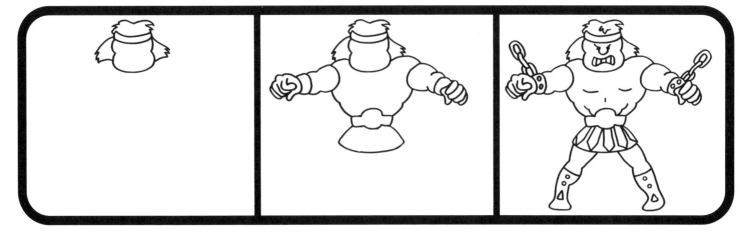

Sitting Bull

Super Strongman

Space Saver

Iron Man

Super Boy

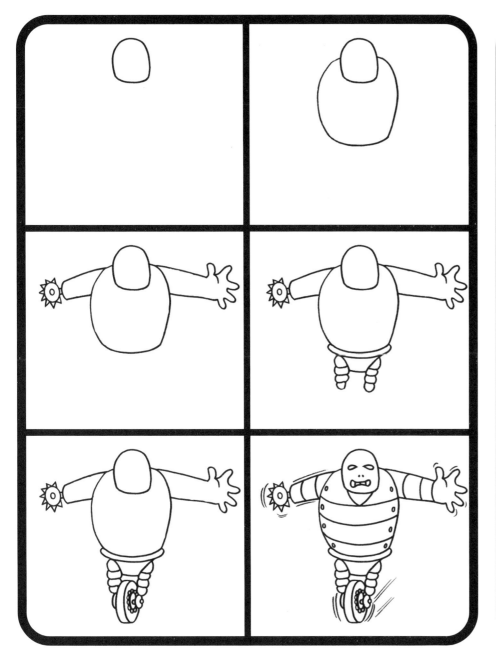

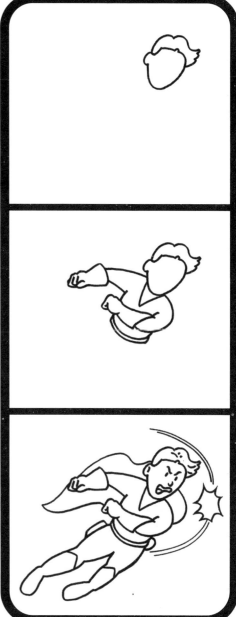

Super Woof

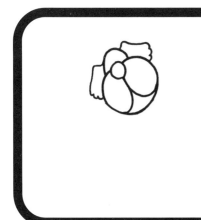  

Super Bunny

Big Beard

Mighty Mog

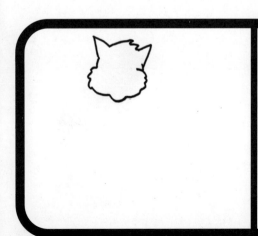